Assessing Quality in the Early Years:
Early Childhood Environment Rating Scale
Extension (ECERS-E)
Four Curricular Subscales

REVISED EDITION

Kathy Sylva   Iram Siraj-Blatchford   Brenda Taggart

Trentham Books

Stoke on Trent, UK and Sterling, USA

Trentham Books Limited

Westview House	22883 Quicksilver Drive
734 London Road	Sterling
Oakhill	VA 20166-2012
Stoke on Trent	USA
Staffordshire	
England ST4 5NP	

First published 2003
Revised edition 2006
Reprinted 2006
Reprinted 2007

British Library Cataloguing-in-Publication Data
A catalogue record for this book is available from the British Library

ISBN-13: 978-1-85856-393-0

Designed and typeset by Trentham Print Design Ltd., Chester and printed in Great Britain by Bemrose Shafron (Printers) Ltd., Chester.

Acknowledgement – *Cover photograph by Helen Tovey for the British Association for Early Childhood Education (Early Education).*

THE EFFECTIVE PROVISION OF PRE-SCHOOL EDUCATION (EPPE) RESEARCH TEAM

PRINCIPAL INVESTIGATORS

Professor Kathy Sylva
Department of Educational Studies, University of Oxford

Professor Edward Melhuish
Institute for the Study of Children, Families and Social Issues, Birkbeck, University of London

Professor Pam Sammons
School of Education, University of Nottingham

Professor Iram Siraj-Blatchford
Institute of Education, University of London

Research Co-ordinator
Brenda Taggart
Institute of Education, University of London

Acknowledgements
Many people have contributed to the development and testing of this instrument. We acknowledge the following, all of whom deserve our thanks: Liz Brooker, Paul Colman, Debby Cryer, Anne Dobson, Bernadette Duffy, Julie Fisher, Marj Jeavons, Lynn Kennington, Katie Lewis, Maria Morahan, Sharon Sadler and John Siraj-Blatchford.

N.B. The EPPE project came to an end in Autumn 2003. The Effective Pre-school and Primary Education Project 3-11 (EPPE 3-11) continues until Autumn 2008. This new study follows the EPPE children to age 11 (the end of their primary education).

Contents

Foreword

It gives me great pleasure to write a foreword to the English Extension to the Early Childhood Environment Rating Scale – Revised (ECERS-R). In planning for the use of the ECERS-R in their research on the Effective Provision of Pre-school Education (EPPE) Project, the authors of the English Extension anticipated the need to expand several of the ECERS items into subscales. These additional subscales were necessary in order to assess areas of emphasis in the English Curriculum Guidance for the Foundation State (3-5+). Before they began work on the Extension, they asked for our advice and ideas, which we were happy to give.

The authors of the English Extension are highly respected experts in the Early Childhood field. They are also valued colleagues of ours, and long time users of the ECERS. At every step of the way, they have shared their work with us and with many others who use the ECERS for research in different countries. The resulting English Extension, which consists of four curricular subscales, is completely in keeping with both the formal aspects and the educational philosophy of the ECERS. The EPPE Project researchers have used the English Extension along with the ECERS-R, and consider the two assessment instruments to be complementary.

I wish to commend the authors of the English Extension on their very careful work and look forward to seeing it in print. I believe it will prove useful in programme assessment in England and beyond.

Professor Thelma Harms
University of North Carolina, Chapel Hill.

Lead author of *Early Childhood Environment Rating Scale – Revised.*
(Harms, Cryer and Clifford, 1998)

Preface to the second edition

The ECERS-E was published in 2003 as a research edition. Our goal was to share the supplementary scales with researchers in the UK and elsewhere who were interested in supplementing the ECERS-R with more fine-grained assessment of curriculum and pedagogy in Early Childhood settings within the English Curriculum Guidance to the Foundation Stage. Although the individual sub-scales bear the titles of curriculum areas such as 'Mathematics' or 'Science/ Environment', the quality ratings within each item are tuned to pedagogy as well as to curriculum and facilities. Across the four sub-scales, each item is scored with reference to pedagogy, resources and the setting's organisation, with discrete indicators usually focusing on one of these at a time. The higher marks are given to settings where there is a balance of child- and adult-initiated activity and a good deal of 'sustained shared thinking' based on a pedagogy of co-construction (Siraj-Blatchford, Sylva, Muttock, Gilden and Bell, DfES Research Report, 2002c). Higher scores across all four sub-scales are also given for evidence of planning and child assessment. Many of the items are scored 3 if the pedagogy seems 'accidental' or lacks coherence. A score of 5 is given if the setting shows evidence of adult instruction balanced with child play and/or exploration. A score of 7 is reserved for pedagogy in which adults and child both contribute to the construction of shared meanings, knowledge and skills. Materials and resources are scored in the same way, with a 3 given for limited although appropriate materials, a 5 given to a wider array of materials and a 7 being reserved for resources suited to the active use of materials by children of differing capabilities, cultural backgrounds, and interests.

Collaboration in development of the second edition

The principal contributors to this revised edition have been Sandra Mathers and Faye Linskey, from the University of Oxford. Their vast experience of using the rating scale in large-scale research studies has been invaluable. They have improved the text, added notes for clarification, and helpful instructions for everyday use. They have transformed a research guide into a practical manual for many different users and for different purposes, including research, institutional self-assessment or for improving pedagogy and curriculum.

This edition has also benefited from the helpful suggestions and queries from around the world, among them from Debby Cryer, Richard Clifford, Thelma Harms, Hans-Guenther Rossbach, Wolfgang Tietze, Eleni Soucacou, Helen Taylor, Emmajane Milton, Frances Charles. We are grateful to everyone who has contributed – but especially to Sandra Mathers and Faye Linskey.

Kathy Sylva
Iram Siraj-Blatchford
Brenda Taggart

January 2006

Introduction to the ECERS-E

The Early Childhood Environment Rating Scale (Harms, Clifford and Cryer, 1998) is an imaginative and sturdy tool for research, self-audit and inspection. It has been used in more than twenty countries – from Singapore to Germany to Chile. Those who use it in countries outside the US often do little more than translate the instrument into the national language, making minor modifications to vocabulary or to types of equipment. This is what has been done in Germany (Tietze, 1996), in the United Kingdom (Sylva *et al*, 1999) and in Portugal (Bairrao, 1996). Elsewhere, as in Tamil Nadu in India, researchers such as Swaminathan (2000) have used the ECERS as a conceptual template on which to build a very different assessment system to suit environments and practices which are far removed from the American Early Childhood Settings in which ECERS was first developed.

In England, the ECERS-R has been found to be appropriate to statutory, private and voluntary settings. It has been used successfully in research (Melhuish 1994; Sylva *et al*, 1999) and to improve practice through self-audit (Siraj-Blatchford, 2002a,b). However, the ECERS-R was developed in the 1980s, based broadly on notions of Developmentally Appropriate Practice (DAP). It adopts a light touch to assessing provision for developing children's emerging literacy, numeracy and scientific thinking. Moreover, it is also light on assessing provision aimed at cultural and intellectual diversity in the setting. The Early Childhood Environment Rating Scale – Extension (ECERS-E) was developed to supplement the ECERS-R by a team of researchers at the Institute of Education, University of London. ECERS-E reflects the English National Early Childhood Curriculum *Curriculum Guidance for the Foundation Stage* (QCA, 2000) as well as the changing notions of Developmentally Appropriate Practice.

Four new sub-scales have been devised for the ECERS-E: Literacy, Mathematics, Science, and Diversity. Items in these sub-scales assess the quality of curricular provision, including pedagogy, in these domains aimed at fostering children's academic development (Sammons *et al,* 2002).

The ECERS-E has been piloted extensively in a variety of settings for predictive validity (Sylva, AERA 2001). A study of 3,000 children in Britain (The Effective Provision of Pre-School Education (EPPE) Project, Institute of Education, University of London) has shown that assessments of their Early Childhood Settings made on the ECERS-E are better predictors of children's intellectual and language progress (3-5 years) than were assessments on the same settings using the ECERS-R. This validation came from a national study carried out in England to explore the relationship between the quality of pre-school measured by the Early Childhood Environment Rating Scale-Revised (ECERS-R) and the developmental progress of more than 3,000 pre-school children. This study is part of the Effective Provision of Pre-school Education (EPPE) project funded by the UK government. The study follows the development of children between entry to pre-school at the age of 3 and entry to school at age 5 years. The predictive validity of the ECERS-R was compared to this extension (ECERS-E), relying on the same format but with more detailed assessment of the 'curricular environment' which is specified in the *English Foundation Stage Curriculum Guidance*, QCA (2000). Scores on the total ECERS-R were not related to cognitive progress over the two year period but the scores on one of its subscales, 'Social Interaction', were positively related to increases in children's **independence** and **cooperation.** For academic development, however, the ECERS-E was significantly related to progress in children's **language**, **non-verbal reasoning**, **number skills**, and **pre-reading skills**. We suggest that quality is not a universal concept but depends on national priorities. If academic achievement is valued at the start of school, then the ECERS-E is a good predictor of readiness for school. But if social outcomes are valued, then the social interaction scale on the ECERS-R may be a better predictor of readiness.

However, we believe both are equally important and therefore recommend that the scales should be used together. ECERS-R is available from Teachers College Press (see Appendix C for ordering information for this and other EPPE publications).

How to use the ECERS-E rating scale

Before using the scale

Before using the ECERS-E scale as a self-assessment tool (see next section), a research instrument or simply for guidance, it is strongly recommended that the user acquire some familiarity with the ECERS-R scale. The Teachers College Press have produced a range of materials to accompany the scales that have been developed for training purposes. These include video extracts and advice on making judgements. These materials can be used for both group and self-instruction. After viewing the training package, users will need to conduct several 'trial' observations in order to familiarise themselves with the content of the items included in the scale. This cannot be done on one observation. Using the scales demands a high degree of understanding about not only the content of the scales but about making sense of what is being observed. In many cases information to complete the scales cannot be readily observed and the user may need to question centre staff, sensitively, about their practices. Any user therefore needs to be familiar with the content of the scales and also to be confident in 'probing' for additional information beyond that which is observed.

Before using the scales, it is strongly recommended that the observer have some external validation conducted on their judgements. This could be done by a colleague or outsider as a measure of inter-rater reliability. This may need to be arranged before the period of observations to ensure that the inter-rater will be available.

Administering the scale
Preparing for the observation.

1   Sufficient time should be put aside to conduct the observations. One half day is recommended. Make sure that the time set aside allowes enough time to talk to staff without children present (usually at the end of the observation) so you can ask any additional questions. It is recommended that you allow approximately fifteen minutes to do this.

2   The room or area in which the observations take place should be clearly defined i.e. is it just the room/provision for 3 year olds which is going to be observed or a whole centre?

3   Before beginning the observation ensure you have completed as much of the identifying information as possible i.e. names of centre, age group observed etc.

4   Spend some time before the observations orientating yourself to the centre and its geography. It is a good idea to find out from the staff what programme of activities is planned during the period of the observation.

5   If you need to see additional paperwork (such as planning documents) to assist you in making a judgement make sure that the staff know you are going to ask to see (or be given copies) of them. Allow sufficient time for staff to get them for you.

6   Make sure that you are clear about the value placed on some of the terms used throughout the scale i.e. 'a few' (Environmental print 3.1) suggests a limited number, probably no more than five, while 'many' (same item 5.1) suggests an amount over ten. Clear distinctions (% value) should be made between 'few', 'some', 'many', 'variety', 'most', 'sometimes', and agreed by the observer and inter-rater. In this context 'easily accessible' (i.e. books and literacy areas) means that children can reach and use materials easily, not necessarily that every child has access at all times. Similarly the term 'staff' refers to all adults who have direct contact with children.

Conducting the observation

1   The items do not have to be administered in the order in which they appear in the booklet. If a cooking activity is taking place you may decide to score this immediately and then come back to other items later on. Some items may be scored more easily than others. Resources, for instance, are easier to observe.

2   Only score an item after you have allowed sufficient time to make a reasoned judgement. This is particularly important for items which demand observing the interactions between adult/child or child/child. You need to be sure that what you are observing is representative of the practices as a whole.

3   Take care not to interrupt the activities being observed. The observer should be a 'fly on the wall' and avoid interacting with the children or staff. It is important to be as unobtrusive as possible and to remain neutral in your actions, expressions and reply to questions.

4   If you are not sure about something, make detailed notes on your scoring sheet and ensure that these are clear enough for you to follow when you come back to them at the end of the observation. This is particularly important if you are using the scales for self-evaluation and plan to give feedback to others on your observations.

5   Make sure you score **all** items at the time of the observation. It is very difficult to record scores away from the setting.

6   A new score sheet should be used for each observation (permission is granted to photocopy score sheets ONLY) and you should make sure that the scoring is both legible and photocopiable. It is recommended that you use a pencil and have a rubber with you to amend scoring as you work.

Scoring the scales

THIS CAN ONLY BE DONE ONCE THE OBSERVER IS FAMILIAR WITH THE SCALE.

1   Read the items carefully, as judgements have to be made exactly in accordance with the instructions given.

2   Scores must reflect the observed practice and not some future plan the centre may have told you about.

3   The scale measures from 1 to 7 with 1 = inadequate, 3 = minimal 5 = good and 7 = excellent.

4   The observation should always start with 1 and be worked though systematically.

5   A rating of 1 must be given if **any** indicator in section 1 is scored YES.

6   A rating of 2 is given when **all** indicators under 1 are scored NO and at least half of the indicators under 3 are scored YES.

7   A rating of 3 is given when **all** indicators under 1 scored NO and **all** indictors under 3 are scored YES.

8   A rating of 4 is given when **all** indicators under 3 are met and at least half of the indicators under 5 are scored YES.

9   A rating of 5 is given when **all** indicators under 5 are scored YES.

10 A rating of 6 is given when **all** indicators under 5 are met and at least half of the indicators under 7 are scored YES.

11 A rating of 7 is given when **all** indicators under 7 are scored YES.

12 A score of NA (Not Applicable) may only be given for indicators or for entire items when this scale is omitted i.e. on maths and science activities where a choice of observed activities is allowed.

13 To calculate average subscale scores, sum the scores for each item in the sub-scale and divide by the number of items scored. The total mean scale score is the sum of all item scores for the entire scale divided by the number of items scored.

N.B. These administrative notes are based on the ECERS-R guidance. We are grateful to the Chapel Hill Team for their assistance in helping us write our guidance notes.

Using ECERS as a self assessment and improvement tool at centre level

Since the publication of the Effective Provision of Pre-School Education (EPPE) Technical Papers which relate quality, as measured by ECERS-R and ECERS-E, with child cognitive and social developmental outcomes, we have been inundated with requests for the ECERS-E document (which was particularly significant for cognitive outcomes – see Introduction) not only in the UK but from around the world. Although we have provided copies of the ECERS-E and given the details of where to purchase ECERS-R in response to these requests, we have been concerned about how this rating scale is used. We have asked people what they have wanted the scale for and most have replied that they want to use it in some way in their early childhood or Foundation Stage settings, or as a research instrument.

As a team we have discussed what it means for people to use the scales when they haven't been trained to do so. We have also been concerned about their use in settings where the general professional training of the staff may be limited. In such circumstances we are sure that critical but constructive support will be needed. We have also been concerned about the lack of external validation, which means that settings can rate themselves as good, excellent, or in need of further development but where there is no real comparative measure.

It was for these reasons that one of us used the ECERS-R and ECERS-E as part of the Early Excellence Evaluations of two centres over a period of two to three years (Siraj-Blatchford, 2002a and 2002b). With the support of the heads and senior teachers, the ECERS were used as a self-development tool by both centres. The centres that trialled this application of the instruments were the Gamesley Early Excellence Centre in Derbyshire and the Thomas Coram and Coram Parents' Early Excellence Centre in London.

All staff were initially provided with a full day's training on what is meant by 'quality', the culturally specific aspects of it as well as what we consider are some universal aspects e.g. treating children with respect, not harming or smacking children. Then the staff were introduced to the ECERS-R and the ECERS-E. The staff were asked to systematically assess the ratings from the scale. on adults and children in different centres shown on video working together. They were given time to compare and discuss their judgements. The training materials produced by Teachers College Press are used, and the training was delivered by a trained researcher/user of the scale. The staff were then asked to trial two of the scales for themselves, working in pairs, and to report back their findings, their agreements and disagreements, during a follow-up half day training session.

During the two years, the staff regularly reported on their discussions and progress with the scales. They found it easier to begin by rating the less threatening subscales such as furnishings and display. From this they learnt that it was the discussions themselves that provided the most useful outcome. These discussions led them to reach agreed meanings for good practice. The staff recommended that each rater should discuss their ratings, done independently but based on the same observations, immediately after the event and compare their ratings and discuss why it was that perceptions sometimes differed. As the staff developed confidence in their rating and discussion, they became more critical of their setting and their practices, and at times also more critical about aspects of the scales. All this was perceived as productive, as most of their observations led to positive actions. For Instance at the Thomas Coram EEC, after rating their Language and Reasoning' subscale, they decided to take action as follows:

Within six months to:

- provide in-service training for all staff on extending children's conversations, focusing on developing the use of open-ended questions.

- establish listening areas in the rooms used by children aged 3 – 5 yrs.

Within a year:

- the need is identified to order more dressing-up clothes and to increase the range and quality of the clothes for socio-dramatic play.

Similarly, after rating the ECERS-R sub-scale on Personal Care Routines, staff at the Gamesley EEC decided the following on the item 'greetings and departures':

Staff felt the organisation of the nursery greeting the parents and children was very good on the whole but some felt the departure in the afternoon meant that some children missed out on the important story session. The staff also felt there wasn't enough time to talk or share information with the parents. *All very rushed.* Parents also have to hunt for their children, as each nursery officer went into a different room for small group/story time. There was intense discussion amongst the staff about ways in which they could improve departure time.

Action taken:

The time of arrival and departure for children who attended nursery in the afternoon was changed. The session used to start at 12.45pm and finish at 3.15pm. Now, instead of going into small groups for story time, all the nursery groups join together for a large group story. The staff read the story on a rota basis. Parents now collect their children from this group. This helps parents know where their children are and gives the nursery staff who are not reading the story time to share information with parents about their child.

Impact:

The story sessions are no longer interrupted and there are opportunities for staff and parents to discuss matters regarding about their children.

In both these centres, examples from the ECERS-R and E were documented and discussed. Actions were decided and taken. There was extensive monitoring of the changes made and the outcomes were recorded and revisited. This developmental work allowed staff to reflect, plan and monitor the children's welfare and learning, and for both centres it became an integral part of the ongoing centre development plans and policies.

After two years of such development, the centre heads agreed to take part in an external validation exercise, where another trained researcher with no prior knowledge of it came into the centre and rated it for its environmental quality, using both the ECERS-R and E. Both centres scored an average of six on each scale, placing them between good and excellent on both. They are continuing to use the scales and are now looking at ITERS (Infant and Toddler Environmental Rating Scale) to engage in self-assessment and the development of their practice with the children who are under 3 years old.

What has been learnt from this experience? The headteachers were interviewed as part of their annual evaluation and both had obviously taken the exercise very seriously. When asked why they undertook this in their centre, they replied:

'It's about being brave enough to be objective, it's about being self-critical and hard on yourself' Bernadette Duffy, Head of Thomas Coram and Coram Parents' Early Excellence Centre.

'The discussion process is the best, we got quite high scores but we could be doing better than even what's measured, we as staff are not entirely happy with this and feel we could go further' Lynn Kennington, Head Gamesley Early Excellence Centre.

Clearly, ECERS can be used effectively as a self-assessment and improvement tool at pre-school centre or reception class level (first year of compulsory schooling) as long as the following criteria are met:

*   Rigorous training is provided on both the quality criteria (definitions and cultural variations) and on the use and the role of the scales.

*   It is recognised that an exercise of this nature requires a critical mass of reflective practitioners within the setting.

*   That a critical friend supports the initiative (an insider e.g. local authority adviser or a representative from Higher Education. In the cases of Gamesley and Thomas Coram cited above, their external evaluator also acted as critical friend).

*   There is a willingness to undergo external validation ('blind' assessment by a trained, reliable assessor).

We are grateful to the staff and the head teachers of Gamesley and Thomas Coram EECs for their time and efforts in using ECERS and for helping us to understand how it can best be used by centres as a self-assessment tool.

General approach

This is an observational scale, and the majority of activities and behaviours will need to be observed to give credit. In some cases, it may be possible to find evidence of activities which have taken place – for example, noting the children's work displayed on the walls, or information from children's records. Planning does not provide evidence, as there is no way of knowing how fully plans are adhered to and how they will be interpreted. Where other observations suggest that an area of learning is implemented well, it may be appropriate to accept planning as evidence for certain items. Do not give credit for activities shown in the planning where your observations on the day do not support the planning evidence.

Where it is appropriate to supplement observation with evidence from other sources, individual items are marked as follows:

P – planning evidence acceptable

D – evidence from displays/ photographic records acceptable

R – evidence from children's records acceptable (includes children's portfolios/folders of completed work)

Q – evidence from questioning acceptable.

Throughout the scale, the word 'staff' is used as a generic term to cover the range of adults who work regularly with children in the setting being observed. This could include volunteers and/or students as well as paid staff members.

Item	Inadequate		Minimal		Good		Excellent
	1	2	3	4	5	6	7

Literacy
Item 1. Environmental print: letters and words*

1.1 No labelled pictures are visible to the children. **	3.1 A few labelled pictures (2-4 examples) are present and visible to children. **	5.1 Many labelled pictures (5 or more examples) are on view to the children. **	7.1 Environmental print is discussed and often relates to objects the children bring to the centre.
1.2 No print (except books) relevant to children is on display.	3.2 Children see some printed words (2-4 examples) e.g. labels on shelves or their own names on their coat pegs or paintings.	5.2 Children are encouraged to recognise printed words in their environment (e.g. their own names on peg labels, print on everyday objects such as food packaging, carrier bags).	7.2 There is discussion of the relationship between the spoken and the printed word (e.g. discussing how a particular spoken word is written down). ##
	3.3 Printed words are prominently displayed e.g. 'welcome' on the door ***	5.3 Children are encouraged to recognise letters in their own names. #	7.3 Children are encouraged to recognise *letters* and words in their environment (e.g. in words on labels or posters).

Notes for clarification

* Environmental print includes all printed words in the child's environment other than books e.g. print on posters, displays, labels on shelves/ drawers/ children's pegs, print on packaging/ clothing/ carrier bags, printed instructions e.g. 'please wash your hands'. These can be handwritten as well as printed.

** Do not count print without pictures. Pictures must be accompanied by text relating to the content of the picture e.g. a poster of a car with 'car' printed below it, pictures *and* a text label to identify the contents of a drawer. The text must be in large enough print for children to read, and to be read from a distance.

*** May be above eye level but children can see it easily.

\# Adults must draw explicit attention to letters in children's names.

\## Discussion must actively involve children

Item	Inadequate		Minimal		Good		Excellent
	1	2	3	4	5	6	7

Item 2. Book and literacy areas

1.1 Books are unattractive and/or not of suitable age level. *	3.1 Some books of different kinds are available.	5.1 A wide range of books is available. ***	7.1 Book area is comfortable (rug and cushions or comfortable seating) and filled with a wide range of books of varied style, content and complexity. #
	3.2 An easily accessible area of the room is set aside for books.	5.2 Book area is used independently by children, outside group reading times.	7.2 Adults encourage children to use books and direct them to the book area.
	3.3 Some reading takes place in the book area. **		7.3 Books are included in learning areas outside the book corner.

Notes for clarification

* This refers to the books themselves and not the way in which they are displayed. Score yes if 50% or more of the books are damaged or of an unsuitable age level.

** This could be during whole group time or informally, by groups or individual children, and with or without adults.

*** For example picture/story books, reference/information books, poetry/nursery rhymes. The selection should include many books with text, and books at a variety of levels to cater for different skills and interests.

This requires variety within the types of book offered e.g. reference books on many different topics, story books about animals, people and imaginary creatures. Sizes and formats should vary.

Item	Inadequate		Minimal		Good		Excellent
	1	2	3	4	5	6	7

Item 3. Adult reading with the children

1.1 Adults rarely read to the children. *

3.1 An adult reads with the children most days. **

3.2 Children are encouraged to join in with repetitive words and phrases in the text (where appropriate).

5.1 Children take an active role in group reading during which the words and / or story are usually discussed.

5.2 Children are encouraged to conjecture about and comment on the text e.g. what do you think (the character) will do next?

7.1 There is discussion about print and letters as well as content.

7.2 There is support material for the children to engage with stories by themselves e.g. tapes, flannel board, displays.

7.3 There is evidence of one to one reading with some children.

Notes for clarification

*   Score yes if no reading with the children is seen during the observation. Reading could be formal or informal, with the whole group, small groups or individual children.

**   Score yes if you observe an adult reading with groups or individual children during the observation.

Item	Inadequate		Minimal		Good		Excellent
	1	2	3	4	5	6	7

Item 4. Sounds in words

1.1 Few or no rhymes or poems are spoken or sung. *	3.1 Rhymes are often spoken or sung by adults to children. * and **	5.1 The rhyming components of songs and rhymes are brought to the attention of children.	7.1 Attention is paid to syllabification of words through clapping games, jumping etc. P
	3.2 Children are encouraged to speak and/or sing rhymes.	5.2 The initial sounds of alliteration in words and /or alliterative sentences are brought to the attention of children (e.g. Peter Piper picked a peck of pickled peppers).	7.2 Some attention is given to linking sounds to letters. P

Notes for clarification

*   Give credit for rhymes spoken or sung with small groups of children as well as whole group activities. Adults must be actively involved. For example, only give credit for taped songs/ rhymes if adults explicitly draw the children's attention to the rhymes e.g. encourage them to sing along.

**   This must be seen during the observation

Item	Inadequate		Minimal		Good		Excellent
	1	2	3	4	5	6	7

Item 5. Emergent writing/mark making*

1.1 There are no materials for children to engage in emergent writing.

1.2 Children never observe staff writing down what they (the children) say.

3.1 Children have access to implements for writing such as pencils and felt tips.

3.2 Children have access to paper appropriate to a writing task, e.g. A4 or telephone pads.

3.3 Children sometimes observe staff writing down what they (the children) say.
D, R

5.1 A place in the setting is set aside for emergent writing. **

5.2 Children often observe staff writing down what they (the children) say.

7.1 As well as pencils and paper, the mark-making area has a theme to encourage children to 'write', e.g. an office.

7.2 The purpose of writing is emphasised, e.g. children are encouraged to 'write' and 'read' to communicate to others what they have produced. ***

7.3 Children's emergent writing is displayed for others to see. D

Notes for clarification

* Emergent writing is young children's spontaneous attempts at translating language into a written form. In its earliest stages it may appear as lines and squiggles, but if asked, children can usually tell you what they have 'written'. As children become more proficient, evidence of letters or numbers begin to emerge from this seemingly random mark making. Children copying what an adult has written is not classed as emergent writing.

** This must be a designated area – it is not enough for children to have access to writing materials which they then take to any available table. The writing area could be a real play area e.g. telephone pad and pens alongside a telephone and computer in a role play 'office'.

*** Examples might include producing cards to take home (e.g. for Mother's Day, Easter, Eid) or writing connected to role play (e.g. labelling parcels in a Post Office, writing a shopping list).

Item	Inadequate		Minimal		Good		Excellent
	1	2	3	4	5	6	7

Item 6. Talking and Listening

1.1 Very little encouragement or opportunity for children to talk to adults.	3.1 Some conversation between adults and children occurs.	5.1 Interesting experiences are planned by adults and drawn upon to encourage talk and the sharing of ideas. * P	7.1 Adults provide scaffolding for children's conversations with them **
1.2 Most verbal attention from adults is of a supervisory nature.	3.2 Children are allowed to talk amongst themselves with some adult intervention (e.g. adults asked closed questions).	5.2 Children are encouraged to answer questions in a more extended way (requiring answers of more than one word).	7.2 Children are often encouraged to talk to each other in small groups, and adults encourage their peers to listen to them. *** P
		5.3 Adults regularly create one-to-one opportunities to talk with children by initiating conversations with individuals.	7.3 Adults regularly use open-ended questions to extend the children's language through talk (e.g. 'what do you think would happen if....?', 'how did you make.....?')
			7.4 Children are encouraged to ask questions. #

Notes for clarification

*   Experiences must be planned by adults and have an explicit focus on communication and the sharing of ideas. 'Non-literacy' activities (e.g. baking, science experiments) can be counted if there is a planned focus on discussion.

**   Adults accept and extend children's verbal contributions in conversation.

*** The emphasis here is on small groups – do not count whole group discussions/circle times when scoring this indicator. The communication should be more focused than simply talking while taking part in a play activity. Examples might include children talking about models they have made or recalling a trip outside the. centre.

\#   Examples might include games such as 'Who Am I?', or an adult saying to a child 'go and try that and if you get stuck come back and ask me'. Also give credit for positive reinforcement when children ask questions e.g. adults take the time to stop and answer questions, giving the message that children's questions are welcome.

Item	Inadequate		Minimal		Good		Excellent
	1	2	3	4	5	6	7

Mathematics – N.B. Items 1 and 2 *MUST* be assessed. After assessing Items 1 and 2 you may then select *EITHER* Item 3 or Item 4 for evidence. You may choose the Item that is most apparent during the observation. This mathematics subscale may require access to planning documents.

Item 1. Counting and the application of counting

1.1 Children rarely take part in activities or routines where counting is used.
* and **

1.2 Very few resources are available to encourage the children to take part in counting activities e.g. conkers, shells, buttons, unifix cubes ***

3.1 A few number activities such as counting books, games, songs or rhymes are used with the children. * and **
P, R

3.2 Numbers are named as part of routine activities. *

3.3 Maths provision includes posters featuring numbers or counting books/games. ***

5.1 Number songs, rhymes, counting books and games are often used with the children. **
P, R (must also be observed)

5.2 Children are encouraged to count objects and to associate the spoken numbers with the numerical concepts. e.g. counting the number of children present at registration, counting out six milk cartons for six children.

5.3 Adults use both cardinal (1,2,3...) and ordinal (1st, 2nd, 3rd ..) numbers when working with the children. #

7.1 All children are actively encouraged to take part in counting objects in a variety of contexts, e.g. role play, snack time, sharing lego. ##

7.2 Activities are planned which encourage one-to-one correspondence both indoors and outdoors and outside the setting. P

7.3 Adults incorporate into their planning working with children on specific number activities, e.g. dice games, dominoes, matching numbers to numbers or numbers to pictures. P

7.4 There is a well-equipped maths area with number games, countable objects and books.

Notes opposite.

24

Notes for clarification

* Number activities could include counting songs/rhymes, counting books, counting games, or computer programs which include counting. In theory, any play activity is acceptable if adults make counting an explicit part of the activity e.g. counting the number of blocks needed to make a tower.

Routine activities are non-play based and might include snack or lunchtime, registration, putting coats on and lining up to go outside, tidying up time. Use of number during routine activities might include, for example, working out how many plates are needed for snack time.

** Rarely (1.1) means once a week or less often. A few (3.1) means once a week or more. Often (5.1) means daily: number activities must be seen during the observation to give credit for this indicator.

*** Resources do not need to be accessible daily.

\# Look for evidence of cardinal numbers being used during everyday activities e.g. 'you can go first', 'who will be first/ second/ third to sit down on the carpet for story, or to tidy away?'

\#\# Several instances should be observed: staff should be looking beyond the obvious situations which lend themselves to counting, and bringing number into a wide range of contexts, both formal and informal and with small groups and individuals as well as the whole group.

Item	Inadequate		Minimal		Good		Excellent
	1	2	3	4	5	6	7

Item 2. Reading and writing simple numbers

1.1 Attention is not paid to the reading and/ or writing of simple numbers. *

3.1 Numbers and the equivalent objects are shown next to each other e.g. the number '3' next to three apples.

5.1 Children are encouraged to read and write simple numbers routinely.
D, P, R

7.1 There are planned classroom activities involving numbers and adults encourage reading and writing numbers in a variety of materials. P, R

1.2 No posters or written numbers are displayed in the room.

3.2 Some children occasionally read and write numbers.
P, D, R

3.3 Children's attention is drawn to written number sequence e.g. by a number line or by talking to the children about a counting book. **

5.2 Materials are available to support children in writing numbers, e.g. wooden numerals or other number shapes. ***

7.2 Written number work is linked to a practical purpose e.g. pricing items in a shop corner, putting the birthday number on a birthday card.
D, P, R

Notes for clarification

* There must be some evidence that staff pay attention to number.

** Adults should draw explicit attention to written numbers in sequence. The numbers should also be spoken aloud so that children associate spoken numbers with the written concepts.

*** These do not need to be accessible daily.

Item	Inadequate		Minimal		Good		Excellent
	1	2	3	4	5	6	7

Select Item 3 or 4 for evidence: choose the most apparent one in the observation.

Item 3. Mathematical activities: Shape and space

Inadequate	Minimal	Good	Excellent
1.1 Shape is rarely commented on in ordinary play or daily routines. *	3.1 Some different shapes are available. **	5.1 A wide variety of shapes are available and adults draw children's attention to specific shape names, e.g. circle, square, triangle, rectangle.	7.1 Many activities and materials are available which encourage children to *generalise* shape across a variety of contexts, e.g. art activities, construction activities, group play arrangements, role play. D, P, R
	3.2 Shapes are named as part of everyday activities. ***	5.2 Staff draw children's attention to shape in their own work e.g. drawings, models.	7.2 Activities develop and extend concepts beyond basic shapes and colours e.g. to include properties of two or three dimensional shapes. D, P, R
	3.3 Shape is an explicit part of some activities indoors. D, R, P (with caution)		7.3 Staff encourage children to understand the properties of different shapes (e.g. three sides of a triangle) and to use this understanding to solve shape puzzles and apply their knowledge to new situations. D, P, R
			7.4 Staff plan activities which demonstrate tessellation in shapes. D, P, R

Notes for clarification

* Score yes if no references to shape are seen during the observation and there is no evidence in display that shape work has been carried out in the past.

** Any resources with different shaped pieces can be counted e.g. blocks with different shaped pieces, shape cutters for cooking/play dough activities.

*** Staff members are not required to use the proper names for shapes to give credit for this indicator: common names are acceptable, such as tube, egg-shaped.

27

Item	Inadequate		Minimal		Good		Excellent
	1	2	3	4	5	6	7

Item 4. Mathematical activities: Sorting, matching and comparing

Children are not encouraged to sort, match or compare objects and materials.	3.1 Some sorting and matching items are available. *	5.1 Activities occur regularly which develop and extend sorting and matching skills e.g. sorting by more than one criterion, sorting in different contexts and/or using objects in the child's everyday environment. ***	7.1 Children are encouraged to identify the characteristics of sets of objects, e.g. to explain why a set of shapes is alike by saying 'They are all circles'.
	3.2 Children sort and/or match by at least one criterion e.g. heavy/light or by colour. P, R	5.2 Characteristics which form the basis for sorting and matching are made explicit by the adults e.g. pointed ends on triangles.	7.2 Language which explores sorting, comparing or matching is used in a variety of contexts across a range of activities e.g. ordering the size of the three bears; using words such as curlier, bigger, heavier.
	3.3 Staff demonstrate sorting, comparing or matching and allow the children to participate. **	5.3 Staff encourage children to use comparative language when matching, comparing or measuring e.g. big, bigger, biggest, bigger/smaller.	7.3 Children are encouraged to complete a sorting/ matching/ comparing activity then repeat using a different criterion (including their own) as the basis for sorting/matching/comparing e.g. arrange hats by size then by shape.

Notes for clarification

*   Examples of items which could be matched/sorted include everyday objects such as collections of natural materials (pebbles, pine cones, shells, leaves) and different shaped resources (e.g. containers for sand/water play, construction kit components) as well as the more commercial 'counting' resources such as counting bears and unifix cubes.

**   This could be an informal activity with a small group of children e.g. encouraging the children to sort by colour when tidying away blocks after free play.

***   'Regularly' means at least 3 to 4 times per week.

Item	Inadequate		Minimal		Good		Excellent
	1	2	3	4	5	6	7

Science and Environment (NB Items 1 and 2 *MUST* be assessed, after assessing Items 1 and 2 you may then select *EITHER* Item 3, Item 4 or Item 5 for evidence. Choose the item that is most apparent during the observation. This science subscale may require access to planning documents.

Item 1. Natural materials*

1.1 There is little access indoors to natural materials (fewer than 3 examples).	3.1 Some natural materials are available to the children indoors (5 or more examples).	5.1 Natural materials are used beyond decoration to illustrate specific concepts, e.g. planting seeds or bulbs to illustrate growth P, D	7.1 Children are encouraged to identify and explore a wide range of natural phenomena in their environment outside the centre and talk about/describe them. P, D
	3.2 Natural materials are accessible outdoors (5 or more examples).	5.2 Through regular activities, children are encouraged to explore the characteristics of natural materials e.g. things that are smooth or rough. ** P, D	7.2 Children are encouraged to bring natural materials into the centre. *** Q
		5.3 Adults show appreciation, curiosity and respect for nature when with children, such as interest in fungi or worms, rather than fear or disgust.	7.3 Children are encouraged to make close observations of natural objects and/or draw them. P, D, R

Notes for clarification

* Natural materials in this item are resources which encourage learning of science. Materials should be in their natural state and recognisable as coming from the natural environment. Examples include: plants; collections of pebbles/pine cones/shells/leaves/fruit/vegetables (count a collection as one item); live animals such as fish, hamsters, stick insects, snails. Do not include general play materials which happen to be natural e.g. lentils/pasta. Only count sand and water if they are used purposefully for the learning of science e.g. floating/sinking, comparing properties of wet/dry sand.

** This could include informal discussion e.g. feeling the texture of a pebble found in the playground. Displays may show evidence of activities which have taken place (e.g. materials displayed, with the comment 'we felt the different materials and decided whether they were rough or smooth').

*** Q:. 'How do you collect the natural materials for your topics and/or displays?' 'Do children every bring in natural materials they are interested in? Could you give me some examples?'

Item	Inadequate		Minimal		Good		Excellent
	1	2	3	4	5	6	7

Item 2. Areas featuring science/science resources

Inadequate	Minimal	Good	Excellent
1.1 No evidence of science resources, displays, books or activities.	3.1 Science provision includes a selection of items e.g. magnets or hand lenses.	5.1 A variety of science equipment is readily available for children to use.**	7.1 A wide range of science equipment is available. #
	3.2 Displays show evidence of seasonal change e.g. pictures of spring, winter, autumn, summer.	5.2 There is evidence of collections of things with similar and/or different properties, e.g. things that roll, stretch, bounce, are made of plastic, of metal. ***	7.2 A range of reference materials is available including books, pictures, charts and photographs.
	3.3 Pictures/posters are displayed which could be used to generate discussion about science in the world around us, e.g. posters of the body, life cycle of a butterfly. *	5.3 Print resources go beyond story books to some reference books or material on science topics.	7.3 A large and stimulating science area is set up for the children to use daily.
			7.4 Science materials feature in other areas of the centre as well as the one set aside for science. ##

Notes for clarification

* Pictures/posters must have a science purpose – posters showing, for example, pets or a woodland scene would not be adequate.

** Variety means more of each type of item (so that several children can use the materials at once) but also a greater variety of items than is required for 3.1. Equipment might include collections of natural materials, magnets, mirrors, hand lenses or containers for collecting mini-beasts. Only give credit for general materials (e.g. funnels/containers/plastic tubes for sand and water play) if there is evidence that these are used for the learning of science. Materials do not need to be accessible to the children at all times, but they must be readily available so that staff can access them when the need arises e.g. if the children find mini-beasts in the playground.

*** There must be evidence that collections have been put together on the basis of their scientific properties and not, for example, because they are all the same colour. Collections do not need to be accessible daily.

As required for 5.1, plus examples of more specialised science materials which relate to specific topics e.g. colour (coloured lenses, colour paddles), light (prisms, light boxes), electricity (batteries, wires).

For example, a seaside role play area which has been supplemented with reference books on seaside creatures, a crab claw and a hand lens so that the children can make close observations.

Item	Inadequate		Minimal		Good		Excellent
	1	2	3	4	5	6	7

Select one of Sections 3, 4 or 5 for evidence: choose the one for which you can find the most detailed evidence. In order to assess the higher levels you must have observed staff interacting with children e.g. at the water/sand trough or other activity area. At these levels, evidence is being sought for engagement with children in scientific processes i.e. close observation, raising questions/making guesses (hypothesising), experimenting (see what happens) and communicating and interpreting results (why has this happened).

Item 3. +Science activities: Science processes: Non-living

1.1 Children are not encouraged to explore aspects of their physical environment, and scientific words and concepts do not feature in discussions (see 3.2 for examples).

3.1 Some science exploration or experiments are carried out by adults or children e.g. ice cubes put out in sun. *
P, D, R

3.2 Scientific words and concepts are mentioned in everyday activities e.g. discussing the weather (is it hot/cold); using the words floating and sinking at the water tray; talking about melting, pressure, why/how things move.

5.1 Staff regularly plan and introduce appropriate scientific concepts (e.g. how materials change, magnetism, sinkers and floaters) and children handle materials.
P, R, D

5.2 Adults draw attention to characteristics and changes in materials e.g. birthday candles melting.

5.3 Children are encouraged to use more than one sense to explore non-living phenomena and talk about their experience (e.g. touch/smell as well as sight).

7.1 Children are encouraged to experience a range of scientific concepts/ideas. * P

7.2 Adults support children in systematically seeking answers.

7.3 All children have hands-on experience in varied science activities. P

7.4 Adults engage the children in discussion about materials and their characteristics and encourage children to ask questions and record results. P

Notes for clarification

* Examples might include: investigating the friction of different surfaces for toy cars; insulation/absorbency of materials e.g. which material will keep our doll the warmest/driest?); changing state of materials e.g. water as a solid, liquid, vapour.

Item	Inadequate		Minimal		Good		Excellent
	1	2	3	4	5	6	7

Item 4. +Science activities: Science processes: Living processes and the world around us

In order to assess the higher levels you must have observed staff interacting with children e.g. in the outdoor area. At these levels, evidence is being sought for engagement with children in scientific processes i.e. close observation, raising questions/making guesses (hypothesising), experimenting (seeing what happens) and communicating and interpreting results (why this has happened).

1.1 Children are not encouraged to explore aspects of their natural environment, and scientific words and concepts do not feature in discussions (see 3.1 and 3.2 for examples).	3.1 Some science exploration or experiments are carried out by adults or children e.g. growing seedlings, keeping tadpoles. P, D, R	5.1 Staff regularly plan and introduce appropriate scientific concepts and children handle materials.	7.1 Adults engage the children in discussion about both plant and animal worlds and their characteristics.
	3.2 Scientific words and concepts are mentioned in everyday activities e.g. plant growth, insect habitats, the cycle of life, caring for living things. *	5.2 Adults draw attention to characteristics and changes in the natural world where appropriate e.g. the life cycle of a butterfly, the ageing process.	7.2 Adults encourage children to ask questions and record results. P, R, D
	3.3 There are living things present, either indoors or outdoors e.g. plants, fish, snails.	5.3 Children are encouraged to use more than one sense to explore living phenomena and talk about their experience (e.g. touch/smell as well as sight).	7.3 All children have hands-on experience with living things where appropriate. P, D

Notes for clarification

*   Examples might include discussing pets owned by the children or looking at a spider found in the playground.

Item	Inadequate		Minimal		Good		Excellent
	1	2	3	4	5	6	7

Item 5. Science activities: Science processes: Food preparation

In order to assess the higher levels you must have observed staff interacting with children e.g. at snack time or during a cooking activity. At these levels, evidence is being sought for engagement with children in scientific processes i.e. close observation, raising questions/making guesses (hypothesising), experimenting (seeing what happens) and communicating and interpreting results (why this has happened).

1.1 No preparation of food or drink is undertaken in front of the children. *	3.1 Food preparation is undertaken by staff in front of the children. *	5.1 Food preparation/cooking activities are regularly provided.	7.1 A variety of cooking activities in which all children may take part are regularly provided. P
	3.2 Some children can choose to participate in food preparation. **	5.2 Most of the children have the opportunity to participate in food preparation.	7.2 The ingredients are attractive and the end result is edible and appreciated, e.g. eaten by children, taken home.
	3.3 Some food-related discussion takes place where appropriate, e.g. staff and children talk about food at snack time, for example, burnt toast, new biscuits or food brought in by the children.	5.3 The staff lead discussion about the food involved and use appropriate language e.g. melt, dissolve. 5.4 Children are encouraged to use more than one sense (feel, smell, taste) to explore raw ingredients.	7.3 The staff lead and encourage discussion on the process of food preparation and/or question children about it e.g. what did it look like before, what does it look like now, what has happened to it?

Notes for clarification

*   This could include routine tasks such as cutting up fruit for snack time as well as planned cooking activities.

Item	Inadequate		Minimal		Good		Excellent
	1	2	3	4	5	6	7

Diversity Item 1: Planning for individual learning needs. Ask to see the records kept on individual children.

1.1 All children in the setting are offered the same range of materials and activities, rather than having activities matched to different ages, capabilities or interests * and **

3.1 Some additional provision is made in terms of developmental stage, or for individuals or groups with specific needs such as learning support or English language support. * and **

5.1 The range of activities provided enables children of all abilities and from all backgrounds to participate in a satisfying and cognitively demanding way, e.g. showing children the different tasks they can attempt with a toy or game. *** P

7.1 The range of activities provided, together with the organisation of social interaction, enables children of all abilities and backgrounds to participate at an appropriate level in both individual and common tasks, e.g. pairing children of different ages and ability for a certain task. #

1.2 No written planning, or planning which takes no account of specific groups or individuals. ** P

3.2 Some of the written planning shows differentiation for particular individuals or groups, e.g. simple peg puzzles up to complex jigsaws, fat paint brushes and watercolour brushes. ** P

5.2 Day to day plans are drawn up with the specific aim of developing activities that will satisfy the needs of each child either individually or as part of a group. P

7.2 Planning sheets identify the role of the adult when working with individuals/pairs/groups of children. Planning also shows a range of capability levels at which a task or activity may be experienced. ## P

Item	Inadequate 1	2	Minimal 3	4	Good 5	6	Excellent 7
	1.3 No records kept, or the records describe only activities and not the children's response or success in that activity, e.g. only ticked checklists or sampling of children's work. R		3.3 Written records indicate some awareness of how individuals have coped with activities, or of the appropriateness of activities, e.g. 'needs bilingual support' 'could only manage to count to 2'. R		5.3 Children are observed regularly, and individual records are kept on their progress in different aspects of their development. R		7.3 Children are observed regularly and their progress is recorded and used to inform planning. R
			3.4 Staff show some awareness of the need to support and recognise children's differences, praising children of all abilities publicly. ###		5.4 Staff consistently draw children's attention to the difference in people in a positive way. ### P, D		7.4 Staff specifically plan activities which draw the attention of the whole group to difference and capability in a positive way, e.g. showing children who are disabled in a positive light, celebrating bilingualism. #### P

Notes for clarification

* There should be evidence that differentiated activities are offered to children within the 3-5 age range.

** Individual planning (known in the UK as Individual Education Plans) may be produced for some children with special needs. However, only give credit for this if there is evidence that they are incorporated into the daily plan of activities.

*** The range of activities should show some differentiation for children with particular needs (e.g. children of different ages/capabilities, children with English as an additional/second language) in addition to those with identified special needs.

\# The focus here is on the organisation of social interaction. It may be necessary to ask about this as it will not always be apparent why children have been encouraged to work together on a task (e.g. Why have you encouraged those children to work together? Do you ever encourage certain children to work together? Why? Can you give some examples?).

\#\# This should be more detailed than simply listing which adult works with which activity/group.

\#\#\# A setting in which staff praise all children regularly would get credit for 3.4, but to give credit for 5.4 attention must be drawn to the difference between people. e.g. an adult discussing with the group at lunchtime why a particular child doesn't eat meat, making it clear that this is an acceptable difference.

\#\#\#\# Also take account of wasted opportunities e.g. times when a child who has special needs does something well that goes unnoted.

Item	Inadequate		Minimal		Good		Excellent
	1	2	3	4	5	6	7

Item 2: Gender equality and awareness

1.2 Where books, pictures, dolls and displays portray gender, most (90% or more) conform to gender stereotypes.

3.1 Some * books, pictures, dolls and displays include images which do not conform to gender stereotypes (e.g. father looking after baby, female police officer).

5.1 Many ** books, pictures, dolls and displays show men and women in non-stereotypical roles (e.g. female doctors or plumbers).

7.1 The children's attention is specifically drawn to books, pictures, dolls and displays that show males and females in non-stereotypical roles, and specific activities are developed to help the children discuss gender. # Q

1.2 The staff ignore or encourage stereotyped gender behaviours, e.g. boys are rarely encouraged to work in the home corner, girls are praised for looking pretty or boys for being strong.

3.2 Children's activities and behaviour sometimes cross gender stereotypes, e.g.. boys cooking or caring for dolls in the home corner, girls playing outside on large mobile toys.

5.2 Children are explicitly encouraged to participate in activities which cross gender boundaries, e.g. all children are expected (not forced) to join in construction and gross-motor play.

7.2 In encouraging both boys and girls to participate equally in all activities, staff are confident in discussing and challenging the stereotypical behaviours and assumptions of children. Are there specific times when certain things can be done **only** by girls or by boys?

5.3 Dressing-up clothes encourage non-stereotyped cross-gender roles, girl **and** boy nurse or police outfits and non-gendered clothing e.g. cook hat/apron, dungarees.

7.3 Male educators are employed to work with children and/ or men are sometimes invited to work in the centre with the children. ***

Notes for clarification

*   11-20% of those which portray gender

**   20-50% of those which portray gender

*** Use questioning if male staff members not present.

\#   Observed examples might include staff reading and discussing stories like *The Paperbag Princess, Mrs Plug the Plumber* which challenge traditional role-models. If non-stereotypical books and resources are present but staff are not observed using them, ask non-leading question such as 'did you choose these resources for a particular reason?' or 'could you give me an example of how you use these books/resources?'

Item	Inadequate		Minimal		Good		Excellent
	1	2	3	4	5	6	7

Item 3: Race equality and awareness

1.1 Books, pictures, dolls and displays show no or little evidence of ethnic diversity in society or the wider world.

3.1 The children sometimes play with toys and artefacts from cultures other than the ethnic majority. * P, D, R

3.2 Books, pictures, dolls and displays show people from a variety of ethnic groups, even if the images are insensitive or stereotyped ** D

5.1 Children play with artefacts drawn from an extensive range of cultures e.g. range of dressing-up clothes, cooking and eating utensils used in dramatic play. ***

5.2 Some books, pictures, dolls and displays show people from different ethnic groups in non-stereotypical roles e.g. as scientists, doctors, engineers.

5.3 Some images/activities show children that they have much in common with people from other cultural groups e.g. images which stress physical similarities, or similarities in rituals and day-to-day activities. # P, D

5.4 Staff intervene appropriately when child or adult in the setting shows prejudice. ## Q

7.1 Staff develop activities with the express purpose of promoting cultural understanding e.g. attention is drawn to similarities and differences in things and people, different cultures are routinely brought into topic work, visitors and performers reflect a range of cultures. ### P

7.2 Specific activities are developed to promote understanding of difference e.g. paints are mixed to match skin tones to visibly show subtleties of difference. ### P

7.3 In multi-ethnic areas ethnic minority educators are employed in the centre. Elsewhere, black and ethnic minority people are sometimes invited into the setting to work with the children. Q

Notes overleaf.

37

Notes for clarification

*   These do not need to be out every day, but there should be evidence that stored/borrowed toys or artefacts (e.g. cooking utensils/ foods, dressing up clothes, musical instruments) from other cultures are sometimes used, for example, to celebrate different festivals.

**   For example: other nationalities portrayed only in national dress, Africans shown in traditional rural setting, black dolls with white features.

***   To give credit for this indicator, there should be evidence of more than occasional 'tokenistic' celebration of other cultures/festivals. Race equality and multicultural awareness should be embedded in the ethos of the setting, and children should receive a constant message that all children do similar everyday things, e.g. go to the park, attend weddings.

\#   Similarities and differences must be explicitly shown in display and/or planning.

\#\#   If no prejudice is shown, use a question such as 'what would you do if one of the children showed prejudice towards another, or made a racist remark?' Give credit for this indicator if the answer indicates sensitive approach: the child should not be blamed, but told that their words and/or behaviour are inappropriate/inaccurate. The adult should then give a correct explanation and suggest more appropriate response.

\#\#\#   To achieve a score of 7 a setting must use activities as a vehicle to take children beyond simple recognition and into understanding and respect of different races and cultures.

Score Sheets

Centre/School_____ Date _____

Observer_____ No. staff present_____

Time observation began_____ Time observation ended_____

No. children enrolled_____ No. children present_____

Age range of children_____ youngest___ oldest.

No. of chld with sp. needs_____

Type of disabilities present: Physical/cognitive/social/emotional

---

LITERACY SUBSCALE

1. Environmental print 1 2 3 4 5 6 7 Code:_____
letters and words

Score:_____

	Y N		Y N		Y N		Y N
1.1	☐ ☐	3.1	☐ ☐	5.1	☐ ☐	7.1	☐ ☐
1.2	☐ ☐	3.2	☐ ☐	5.2	☐ ☐	7.2	☐ ☐
		3.3	☐ ☐	5.3	☐ ☐	7.3	☐ ☐

Notes:

2. Book and 1 2 3 4 5 6 7 Code:_____
literacy areas

Score:_____

	Y N		Y N		Y N		Y N
1.1	☐ ☐	3.1	☐ ☐	5.1	☐ ☐	7.1	☐ ☐
		3.2	☐ ☐	5.2	☐ ☐	7.2	☐ ☐
						7.3	☐ ☐

Notes:

3. Adult reading 1 2 3 4 5 6 7 Code:_____
with the children

Score:_____

	Y N		Y N		Y N		Y N
1.1	☐ ☐	3.1	☐ ☐	5.1	☐ ☐	7.1	☐ ☐
		3.2	☐ ☐	5.2	☐ ☐	7.2	☐ ☐
						7.3	☐ ☐

Notes:

4. Sounds in words 1 2 3 4 5 6 7 Code:_____

Score:_____

	Y N		Y N		Y N		Y N
1.1	☐ ☐	3.1	☐ ☐	5.1	☐ ☐	7.1	☐ ☐
		3.2	☐ ☐	5.2	☐ ☐	7.2	☐ ☐

Notes:

5. Emergent writing/ 1 2 3 4 5 6 7 Code:_____
mark making

Score:_____

	Y N		Y N		Y N		Y N
1.1	☐ ☐	3.1	☐ ☐	5.1	☐ ☐	7.1	☐ ☐
1.2	☐ ☐	3.2	☐ ☐	5.2	☐ ☐	7.2	☐ ☐
						7.3	☐ ☐

Notes:

6. Talking and 1 2 3 4 5 6 7 Code:_____
listening

Score:_____

	Y N		Y N		Y N		Y N
1.1	☐ ☐	3.1	☐ ☐	5.1	☐ ☐	7.1	☐ ☐
1.2	☐ ☐	3.2	☐ ☐	5.2	☐ ☐	7.2	☐ ☐
				5.3	☐ ☐		

Notes:

ASSESSING QUALITY IN THE EARLY YEARS

A. Subscale (Items 1-6) Score_____

B. Number of items scored_____

LITERACY SUBSCALE average score (A÷B)_____

MATHEMATICS SUBSCALE

1. Counting   1 2 3 4 5 6 7   Code:_____

    Y N   Y N NA   Y N   Y N   Score:_____

1.1 ☐ ☐   3.1 ☐ ☐ ☐   5.1 ☐ ☐   7.1 ☐ ☐
1.2 ☐ ☐   3.2 ☐ ☐ ☐   5.2 ☐ ☐   7.2 ☐ ☐
       3.3 ☐ ☐ ☐   5.3 ☐ ☐   7.3 ☐ ☐
                          7.4 ☐ ☐

Notes:

---

2. Reading and writing 1 2 3 4 5 6 7   Code:_____
    simple numbers
                                 Score:_____

   Y N   Y N   Y N   Y N
1.1 ☐ ☐   3.1 ☐ ☐   5.1 ☐ ☐   7.1 ☐ ☐
1.2 ☐ ☐   3.2 ☐ ☐   5.2 ☐ ☐   7.2 ☐ ☐
      3.3 ☐ ☐

Notes:

---

3. Shape and space 1 2 3 4 5 6 7   Code:_____

   Y N   Y N   Y N   Y N   Score:_____
1.1 ☐ ☐   3.1 ☐ ☐   5.1 ☐ ☐   7.1 ☐ ☐
      3.2 ☐ ☐   5.2 ☐ ☐   7.2 ☐ ☐
      3.3 ☐ ☐   7.3 ☐ ☐
                      7.4 ☐ ☐

Notes:

---

4. Sorting, matching 1 2 3 4 5 6 7   Code:_____
    and comparing
   Y N   Y N   Y N   Y N   Score:_____
1.1 ☐ ☐   3.1 ☐ ☐   5.1 ☐ ☐   7.1 ☐ ☐
      3.2 ☐ ☐   5.2 ☐ ☐   7.2 ☐ ☐
      3.3 ☐ ☐   5.3 ☐ ☐   7.3 ☐ ☐

Notes:

A. Subscale (Items 1-4) Score_____

B. Number of items scored_____

MATHEMATICS SUBSCALE average score (A÷B)_____

Notes:

SCIENCE SUBSCALE	

1. Natural materials   1   2   3   4   5   6   7   Code:_____

	Y N		Y N		Y N		Y N	Score:_____
1.1 ☐ ☐	3.1 ☐ ☐	5.1 ☐ ☐	7.1 ☐ ☐					
	3.2 ☐ ☐	5.2 ☐ ☐	7.2 ☐ ☐					
		5.3 ☐ ☐	7.3 ☐ ☐					

Notes:

---

2. Science resourcing   1   2   3   4   5   6   7   Code:_____

	Y N		Y N		Y N		Y N	Score:_____
1.1 ☐ ☐	3.1 ☐ ☐	5.1 ☐ ☐	7.1 ☐ ☐					
	3.2 ☐ ☐	5.2 ☐ ☐	7.2 ☐ ☐					
	3.3 ☐ ☐	5.3 ☐ ☐	7.3 ☐ ☐					
			7.4 ☐ ☐					

Notes:

---

3. +Science processes: 1   2   3   4   5   6   7   Code:_____
Non Living

	Y N		Y N		Y N		Y N	Score:_____
1.1 ☐ ☐	3.1 ☐ ☐	5.1 ☐ ☐	7.1 ☐ ☐					
	3.2 ☐ ☐	5.2 ☐ ☐	7.2 ☐ ☐					
		5.3 ☐ ☐	7.3 ☐ ☐					
			7.4 ☐ ☐					

Notes:

---

3. Science processes: 1   2   3   4   5   6   7   Code:_____
Non Living

	Y N		Y N		Y N		Y N	Score:_____
1.1 ☐ ☐	3.1 ☐ ☐	5.1 ☐ ☐	7.1 ☐ ☐					
	3.2 ☐ ☐	5.2 ☐ ☐	7.2 ☐ ☐					
		5.3 ☐ ☐	7.3 ☐ ☐					
			7.4 ☐ ☐					

Notes:

---

4. Science processes: 1   2   3   4   5   6   7   Code:_____
Living processes

	Y N		Y N		Y N		Y N	Score:_____
1.1 ☐ ☐	3.1 ☐ ☐	5.1 ☐ ☐	7.1 ☐ ☐					
	3.2 ☐ ☐	5.2 ☐ ☐	7.2 ☐ ☐					
	3.3 ☐ ☐	5.3 ☐ ☐	7.3 ☐ ☐					

Notes:

---

5. Science processes: 1   2   3   4   5   6   7   Code:_____
Food preparation

	Y N		Y N		Y N		Y N	Score:_____
1.1 ☐ ☐	3.1 ☐ ☐	5.1 ☐ ☐	7.1 ☐ ☐					
	3.2 ☐ ☐	5.2 ☐ ☐	7.2 ☐ ☐					
	3.3 ☐ ☐	5.3 ☐ ☐	7.3 ☐ ☐					
		5.4 ☐ ☐	7.4 ☐ ☐					

Notes:

A. Subscale (Items 1-5)   Score_____

B. Number of items scored_____

SCIENCE AND ENVIRONMENT average score (A÷B)_____

3. Race equality and awareness

  1   2   3   4   5   6   7   Code:_____

	Y N	Y N	Y N	Y N	Score:_____
1.1	☐ ☐	3.1 ☐ ☐	5.1 ☐ ☐	7.1 ☐ ☐	
		3.2 ☐ ☐	5.2 ☐ ☐	7.2 ☐ ☐	
			5.3 ☐ ☐	7.3 ☐ ☐	
			5.4 ☐ ☐	7.4 ☐ ☐	

Notes:

DIVERSITY SUBSCALE

1. Individual learning 1   2   3   4   5   6   7   Code:_____
 needs

	Y N	Y N	Y N	Y N	Score:_____
1.1	☐ ☐	3.1 ☐ ☐	5.1 ☐ ☐	7.1 ☐ ☐	
1.2	☐ ☐	3.2 ☐ ☐	5.2 ☐ ☐	7.2 ☐ ☐	
1.3	☐ ☐	3.3 ☐ ☐	5.3 ☐ ☐	7.3 ☐ ☐	
		3.4 ☐ ☐	5.4 ☐ ☐	7.4 ☐ ☐	

Notes:

A. Subscale (Items 1-3)   Score_____

B. Number of items scored_____

DIVERSITY SUBSCALE average score (A÷B)_____

2. Gender equality and awareness

  1   2   3   4   5   6   7   Code:_____

	Y N	Y N	Y N	Y N	Score:_____
1.1	☐ ☐	3.1 ☐ ☐	5.1 ☐ ☐	7.1 ☐ ☐	
1.2	☐ ☐	3.2 ☐ ☐	5.2 ☐ ☐	7.2 ☐ ☐	
			5.3 ☐ ☐	7.3 ☐ ☐	

Notes:

TOTAL AND AVERAGE SCORE

	Score	Items scored	Av. score
Literacy subscale	_____	_____	_____
Mathematics	_____	_____	_____
Science and environment	_____	_____	_____
Diversity	_____	_____	_____

ECERS-E Profile

Centre/ School _____   Observer 1 (date)_____   Observer 1_____

Teacher/Classroom_____   Observer 2 (date)_____   Observer 2_____

	1	2	3	4	5	6	7	
1. Environmental print								Language Subscale
2 Book and literacy areas								Average Subscale Score
3 Adult reading with child								Observer 1 =
4 Sounds in words								Observer 2 =
5 Emergent writing								
6 Talking and listening								
1 Counting								Mathematics Subscale
2 Reading and writing numbers								Average Subscale Score
3 Shape and space								Observer 1 =
4 Matching, sorting and comparing								Observer 2 =
1 Natural materials								Science Subscale
2 Science resources								Average Subscale Score
3 Non-living								Observer 1 =
4 Living								Observer 2 =
5 Food preparation								
1 Planning for individual needs								Diversity - Average Subscale Score
2 Gender equality and awareness								Observer 1 =
3 Race equality and awareness								Observer 2 =

Appendix A: Overview of the Subscales and Items of the ECERS-R

Space and Furnishings

1	Indoor space
2	Furniture and routine care, play and learning
3	Furnishing for relaxation and comfort
4	Room arrangement for play
5	Space for privacy
6	Child-related display
7	Space for gross motor play
8	Gross motor equipment

Personal care routines

9	Greeting/departing
10	Meals/snacks
11	Nap/rest
12	Toileting/diapering
13	Health practices
14	Safety practices

Language and Reasoning

15	Books and pictures
16	Encouraging children to communicate
17	Using language to develop reasoning skills
18	Informal use of language

Activities

19	Fine motor
20	Art
21	Music/movement
22	Blocks
23	Sand/water
24	Dramatic play
25	Nature/science
26	Math/number
27	Use of TV, video and/or computers
28	Promoting acceptance of diversity

Interaction

29	Supervision of gross motor activities
30	General supervision of children (other than gross motor)
31	Discipline
32	Staff-child interactions
33	Interactions among children

Programme Structure

34	Schedule
35	Free play
36	Group time
37	Provision for children with disabilities

Parents and Staff

38	Provision for parents
39	Provision for personal needs of staff
40	Provision for professional needs of staff
41	Staff interaction and cooperation
42	Supervision and evaluation of staff
43	Opportunities for professional growth

Appendix B
Reliability and validity of the scales

I. Reliability and validity of ECERS-R

ECERS-R is a revision of the well-known and established original ECERS scale. It maintains the same conceptual framework as well as the same basic scoring approach and administration. As the original version has a long history of research and since demonstrating that quality as measured by the ECERS has good predictive validity (i.e., Peisner-Feinberg and Burchinal, 1997; Whitebook, Howes and Phillips, 1989) the revised version was expected to maintain that form of validity. However, research on the revised instrument reported here indicates predictive validity.

Have the changes to the scale affected the inter-rater reliability? An extensive set of field tests of the ECERS-R was conducted in the spring and summer of 1997 in 45 classrooms (reported in Sylva *et al*, 1999). The authors were not satisfied with the inter-rater reliabilities obtained and decided that further revision was needed. Data from the first exercise were used to determine the changes required to obtain a fully reliable instrument. Substantial revisions were made to the first field-test draft of the scale, using the indicator-level reliabilities as a guide to focus the training process. After the revisions were made, a second test, focusing on inter-rater reliability, was conducted in a sample of 21 classrooms, equally distributed among high-, medium-, and low-scoring rooms in the initial test. Even though this test was conservative, with minimal chances to develop reliability through the discussions that customarily take place following a practice observation, the results of the second test were satisfactory.

Overall, the ECERS-R is reliable at the indicator and item level, and at the level of the total score. The percentage of agreement across the full 470 indicators in the scale is 86.1%, with no item having an indicator agreement level below 70%. At the item level, the proportion of agreement was 48% for exact agreement and 71% for agreement over one point. Perhaps the most appropriate measure of reliability on a scale such as the ECERS is the Kappa, which takes into account the distance between scores given by two independent raters, rather than simple agreement or non-agreement. Kappas of 0.50 and higher are considered acceptable. All the inter-rater weighted Kappas had scores over .50; most were much higher. Only Item 17: Using language to develop reasoning skills, had a Kappa in the low range. For the entire scale, the correlations between the two observers were .92 product moment correlation (Pearson) and .865 rank order (Spearman). The interclass correlation was .92. These figures are all within the generally accepted range, with the total levels of agreement being quite high. These overall figures are comparable with the levels of agreement in the original ECERS.

Internal consistency of the scale at the subscale and total score levels was also examined. Subscale internal consistencies range from .71 to .88 with a total scale interval consistency of .92. These levels of internal consistency indicate that the subscales and total scale can be considered to form reasonable levels of internal agreement providing support for them as separate constructs.

However, many questions regarding reliability and validity remain unanswered because there have not been enough studies to establish the psychometric properties of ECERS-R. Some of the most recent studies have reported inter-rater reliability figures but no other reliability measurements have been taken (such as test-retest or internal consistency measurements). A study in Philadelphia (Jaeger and Funk, 2001) on the quality of child care reports mean inter-rater reliability .92 (.87 to .97) and mean percent agreement within one rating point 93.5% (83% to 100%). A similar mean percent agreement within one rating point (91.1%) is also reported by another study in Connecticut (Gilliam, 2000); while other researchers managed to establish an overall inter-rater agreement of 84% on the ECERS-R before the start of data collection (de Kruif *et al*, 2000). In summary, the field tests in the US revealed acceptable levels of inter-rater agreement at the three levels of scoring-indicators, items and total score. In addition, there is support for using the scores of the sub-scales and the total score to represent meaningful aspects of the environment.

Moreover the validity of ECERS-R has not been fully established independently of ECERS; that is most researchers anticipate ECERS-R to maintain the good validity characteristics that the ECERS has already demonstrated. Studies will be required to answer questions such as: To what degree does the revised version maintain the same magnitude of score as the original version? And do the two versions both predict child development outcomes similarly?

The EPPE study validated the use of ECERS-R for the UK (Sammons *et al*, 2002). Based on data from141 centres, the ECERS-R was associated with the Caregiver Interaction Scale (CIS), which is also a measure of setting quality, to provide information on the construct validity of the ECERS-R. Significant moderate correlations were found between the average total ECERS-R score and two subscales of the CIS (r.58 for the Positive Relationship subscale and r:-.49 for the Detachment subscale). The other two subscales of CIS, Punitiveness and Permissiveness, were also significantly correlated to ECERS-R total in the expected direction: -.23 and -.33 respectively. Especially strong were the correlations between the ECERS-R subscales language and reasoning and social interaction and the CIS subscales positive relationship and detachment (from .48 to .68).

The same study also examined the predictive validity of the ECERS-R in relation to cognitive and behavioural outcomes of 3,000 children in a national study (Sammons *et al*, 2002; Sammons *et al*, in press). Children's cognitive progress was assessed with the British Ability Scales (BAS II; Elliott, Smith, and McCulloch, 1996) administered when the children entered pre-school and when the children entered primary school (at the beginning of reception class). The social and behavioural development was assessed by the Adaptive Social and Behaviour Inventory (Hogan, Scott, and Baurer, 1992). The ECERS-R, either as a total score or a subscale score, was not related to cognitive progress on a number of measures (pre-reading, early number concepts, language, non-verbal reasoning and spatial awareness/reasoning), controlling for a wide range of child, parent, family, home and other pre-school characteristics. The only statistically significant positive effect was associated with the social interaction subscale and the early number concepts. But there were several significant associations between the ECERS-R and the behavioural development measures. There was a significant positive effect associated with the co-operation and conformity subscale and a) the ECERS-R average total, b) the language and reasoning subscale, and c) the social interaction subscale. This last subscale was also positively associated with children's independence and concentration.

As for the factor structure of ECERS-R, although there has not yet been a confirmatory factor analysis to support the item and subscale structure and content of the instrument, two studies have conducted principal components analysis to identify the underlying dimensions that explain the scores in the ECERS-R.

Holloway and her colleagues (2001) used data collected from 92 centres. Their analysis came up with 12 (out of 42 items) principal components with an eigenvalue larger than one. Subsequent analyses with rotation suggested the use of just the first principal component which explained 25.57% of the total variance. The items that loaded on this first component were variable, mainly representing the dimensions of space, materials and interactions. The results are not consistent with previous research on the original ECERS, usually which has provided two factors, one focusing on the teaching aspect of environments and one on the provision of opportunities aspect (Rossbach, Clifford and Harms, 1991; Whitebook, Howes and Phillips, 1989).

Principal components analysis conducted by Sylva and her colleagues (1999) on the 141 centres of the EPPE study resulted in a two-factor solution for the ECERS-R. The first factor is called Activities and Facilities and accounts for over 30% of the variance. The second is Communication and Supervision and can explain 7% of the variance in the scores. The analysis ended up with 11 factors that had an eigenvalue larger than one, but the first two were clearly standing out from the rest, explaining together about 38% of the total variance. The items that loaded more strongly on these two factors can be seen in Table 1.

Table 1 ECERS-R items with the higher loadings on the two factors

Factor 1	Loading	Factor 2	Loading
Sand/Water	0.762	General supervision of children	0.816
Opportunities for personal growth	0.736	Discipline	0.807
Art	0.724	Staff-child interactions	0.742
Child related displays	0.711	Informal use of language	0.741
Blocks	0.656	Language to develop reasoning skills	0.661
Provision for professional needs for staff	0.619	Interactions among children	0.645
Provision for personal needs for staff	0.608		

Clearly, the two-factor solution of the EPPE analysis is closer to the factor structure found in ECERS. Clifford and his colleagues (1998) conducted a confirmatory factor analysis on the ECERS using data obtained from the US, Germany, Portugal and Spain. They confirmed the presence of two factors: the first, called Teaching and Interaction, is very similar to the second factor of the EPPE study, and the factor called Space and Materials closely resembles the first factor of the EPPE study. In both studies internal consistency in each factor was very high, around .9.

In addition, larger data sets will be required to examine empirically the factor structure of the scale. Further research will be needed to determine the extent to which the ECERS-R reveals the same empirical dimensions as the original ECERS. Before turning to reliability and validity of ECER-E, there follows a brief summary of important studies using the previous version of ECERS.

Previous studies using the former ECERS (before revision to ECERs-R)

Many studies all over the world have used the ECERS to describe education and care processes (Farquhar, 1989; Hagekull and Bohlin, 1995; Lera, Owen, and Moss, 1996; Rossbach, Clifford, and Harms 1991), Scarr, Eisenberg, and Deter-Deckard, 1994; Tietze *et al*,1996; and Whitebook, Howes and Pillips, 1989). In all the various countries where the scale has been used, it has proven to be reliable and valid with minor adaptations, suggesting that children from various background 'require similar inputs for success in developmental areas valued in western industrialized countries' (Harms, Clifford, and Cryer, 2002). A further group of studies have demonstrated that the quality characteristics measured in ECERS are significantly related to children's developmental outcomes (Beller *et al,* 1996; Cost, Quality and Child Outcomes in Child Care Centre Research Team, 1995; Kwan, Sylva and Reeves, 1998: Kwan, 1997; McCartney, 1984; Peisner-Feinberg and Burchinal, 1997; Phillips, McCartney and Scarr, 1987; Phillips, Scarr and McCartney, 1987).

II. Reliability and validity of ECERS-E

In the Sylva *et al* study (1999) the relationship between ECERS-R and ECERS-E was also examined. The correlation coefficient was 0.78, indicating a strong positive relationship between the two measures. Even though the two instruments focus on different dimensions of the pre-school settings, they both measure a general construct of 'quality'. Therefore, it is expected that centres obtaining a high score on the ECERS-R will also obtain a high score on the ECERS-E.

Inter-rater reliability on the ECERS-E was calculated from data obtained from the same 25 randomly chosen centres that were used in the reliability analysis of the ECERS-R (Sylva *et al*,1999). The reliability coefficients were calculated separately for separate regions, both percentages of exact agreement between the raters and as a weighted Kappa coefficient. The percentages of inter-rater agreement range from 88.4 to 97.6 and the Kappas range from 0.83 to 0.97, indicating very high levels of agreement between raters.

Factor analysis conducted on the ECERS-E in 141 centres (Sylva *et al*, 1999) indicated the presence of two factors that together account for about 50% of the total variance in the scores. The first factor is called Curriculum Areas and the second Diversity. Table 2 presents the items that load more strongly (higher than .6) on these two factors.

Table 2 ECERS-E items with the higher loading on the two factors

Factor 1	Loading	Factor 2	Loading
Environmental print letters and words	0.684	Gender equity	0.763
Natural materials	0.683	Race equality	0.702
Counting	0.678	Book and literacy areas	0.643
Science resourcing	0.656		
Talking and listening	0.649		
Sounds in words	0.634		

Cronbach's alpha was calculated for each factor and was high for factor 1 (0.84) but moderate for factor 2 (0.64). So internal reliability is high only for the first factor, indicating that more factor analyses on the ECERS-E are needed in order to support the factor structure provided by the EPPE study.

Construct and predictive validity of the ECERS-E scale for the UK have been successfully demonstrated by the same study on 141 pre-school settings (Sylva *et al,* 1999; Sammons *et al,* 2002; Sammons *et.al,* in press). Apart from the high correlation between the ECERS-E and the ECERS-R, construct validity of this new scale has also been established through the strong relationship with the CIS, a scale for assessing the relationships between setting staff and children. Sammons and her colleagues (2002) report significant moderate correlations between the ECERS-E average total and Positive Relationship (*r*=.59) and Detachment (*r*=.-45), two CIS subscales. All correlations were in the expected direction and the correlation coefficients between all the ECERS-E subscales and the CIS subscales ranged from low to moderate, with the positive relationship subscale being moderately associated with all ECERS-E subscales (from .45 to .58).

The predicative validity of the ECERS-E in relation to cognitive progress was found to be better than the power of ECERS-R in the EPPE study on 3,000 children. Controlling for a large number of child, parent, family, home and pre-school characteristics, the ECERS-E average total was significantly associated in a positive direction with pre-reading scores, early number concepts and non-verbal reasoning. The literacy subscale had a significant positive effect both on pre-reading and on early number concepts. In addition, non-verbal reasoning was significantly affected in a positive direction by the maths subscale of the ECERS-E, the diversity subscale and almost significantly by the science and environment subscale. The diversity subscale had also a significant positive effect on early number concepts. As for the behavioural outcomes, although just missing significance at .05 trends of the average total ECERS-E were positive on two of the measures of social/behavioural development: independence/concentration and co-operation/conformity (Sammons *et al*, in press).

III Quality across nations and cultures
Quality is not a universal concept but depends on national curricula and cultural priorities. The outcomes deemed important in children's development will relate in different ways to the many measures of quality. If academic achievement is valued at the start of school, then the ECERS-E is a good predictor of children's readiness for school. This readiness includes language, numeracy skill and the component skills of early literacy. But if social outcomes are valued, then the social interaction scale on the ECERS-R may be a better predictor of a child's good start at school. The social outcomes related most to the processes observed in the ECERS-R were children's independence and cooperation/conformity.

Appendix C: Ordering Information
The Effective Provision of Pre-School (EPPE) Project Technical Papers and ECERS-R

Tech. Paper 1   *An Introduction to the Effective Provision of Pre-school Education (EPPE) Project*   ISBN 085473 591 7 **Autumn 1999**
£8.50

Tech. Paper 2   *Characteristics of the EPPE Project sample at entry to the study*   ISBN 085473 592 5 **Autumn 1999 £4.00**

Tech. Paper 3   *Contextualising EPPE: Interviews with Local Authority co-ordinators and centre managers*   ISBN 085473 593 3 **Autumn 1999 £3.50**

Tech. Paper 4   *Parent, family and child characteristics in relation to type of pre-school and socio-economic differences.*   ISBN 085473 594 1 **Autumn 1999 £4.00**

Tech. Paper 5   *Characteristics of the Centre in the EPPE Study: (Interviews)*   ISBN 085473 595 X **Autumn 2000 £5.00**

Tech. Paper 6   *Characteristics of the Centres in the EPPE Sample: Observational Profiles*   ISBN 085473 596 8 **Autumn 1999 £8.50**

Tech. Paper 6a   *Characteristics of Pre-School Environments*   ISBN 085473 597 6 **Autumn 1999 £8.50**

Tech. Paper 7   *Social/behavioural and cognitive development at 3-4 years in relation to family background*   ISBN 085473 598 4 **Spring 2001**
£5.00

Tech. Paper 8a   *Measuring the Impact of Pre-School on Children's Cognitive Progress over the Pre-School Period*   ISBN 085473 599 2 **Autumn 2002 £8.50**

Tech. Paper 8b   *Measuring the Impact of Pre-School on Children's Social/Behavioural Progress over the Pre-School Period*   ISBN: 085473 683 2 **Spring 2003   £8.50**

Tech. Paper 9   *Report on age 6 assessment*   ISBN: 085473 600 X **Autumn 2004 £5.50**

Tech. Paper 10   *Intensive study of selected centres*   ISBN: 085473 601 8 **Autumn 2003 £11.00**

Tech. Paper 11   *Report on the continuing effects of pre-school education at age 7*   ISBN: 085473 602 6 **Autumn 2004 £5.50**

Tech. Paper 12   *The final report*   ISBN: 085473 603 4 **Autumn 2004 £5.50**

Related Publications

The Early Childhood Environment Rating Scale: Revised Edition (1998). Harms, Clifford and Cryer
ISBN: 08077 3751 8 Available from Teachers College Press. Columbia University. 1234 Amsterdam Avenue. New York. NY10027

Ordering information – For other EPPE Publications

The Bookshop at the Institute of Education. 20, Bedford Way. London WC1H OAL. Tele: 00 44 (0) 207 612 6050 Fax: 0207 612 6407 e-mail: ioe@johnsmith.co.uk website: www.johnsmith.co.uk/ioe or The EPPE Office. The University of London, Institute of Education. 20 Bedford Way, London. WC1H OAL. U.K.Telephone 00 44 (0) 207 612 6219 / Fax. 00 44 (0) 207 612 6230 / e-mail b.taggart@ioe.ac.uk Please Note: Prices will vary according to size of publication and quantities ordered.
Visit the EPPE Website on: www.ioe.ac.uk/projects/eppe

References

Beller, K., Stahnke, M., Butsz, P., Stahl, W. and Wessels, H. (1996). Two measures of the quality of group care for infants and toddlers. *European Journal of Psychology of Education*, 11(2), 151-167.

Clifford, R.M., Burchinal, M.R., Harms, T., Rossbach, H.G. and Lera, M.J. (1998). *Factor structure of the Early Childhood Environment Rating Scale (ECERS): An international comparison.* Chapel Hill, N.C.: Frank Porter Graham Child Development Center.

Cost, Quality and Child Outcomes in Child Care Research Center Research Team (1995). *Cost, quality and child outcomes in child care settings: Public Report.* Denver: Department of Economics, Center for Research and Social Policy, University of Colorado at Denver.

De Kruif, R.E.L., McWilliam, R.A., Ridley, S.M. and Wakely, M.B. (2000). Classification of teachers' interaction behaviours in early childhood classrooms [Electronic version]. *Early Childhood Research Quarterly*, 15(2), 247-268.

Elliott, C.D., Smith, P.and McCulloch, K. (1996). *British Ability Scales Second Edition.* (BAS II). Windsor, Berks: NFER-Nelson.

Farquhar, S. (1989. Assessing New Zealand child day care quality using the Early Childhood Environment Rating Scale. *Early Childhood Development and Care,* 47, 93-105.

Gilliam, W.S. (2000). *The School Readiness Initiative in South-Central Connecticut: Classroom quality, teacher training, and service provision.* Final Report of findings for fiscal year 1999. Retrieved December 2, 2002 from http://nieer.org/resources/research/CSRI1999.pdf

Hagekull, B.and Bohlin, G. (1995). Day care quality, family and child characteristics and socioemotional development. *Early Childhood Research Quarterly,* 10(4), 505-526.

Harms, T., Clifford, R.M.and Cryer, D. (1998) *Early Childhood Environmental Rating Scale, Revised Edition* (ECERS-R), Teachers College Press.

Harms, T., Clifford, R.M. and Cryer, D. (2002). Introduction to the Harms, Clifford and Cryer Early Childhood Environment Rating Scales. Retrieved December 4, 2002 from http://www.fpg.unc.edu/~ecers/intro_frame.html

Harms, T., Clifford, R.M. and Cryer, D. (2003) *Infant/Toddler Environmental Rating Scale-Revised* (ITERS-R) Teachers College Press.

Harms, T., Jacobs., E.V., and White, D.R. (1996) *School-Age Care Environmental Rating Scale* (SACERS) Teachers College Press.

Hogan, A.E., Scott, K.G.and Baurer, C.R. (1992). The Adaptive Social Behaviour Inventory (ASBI): A new assessment of social competence in high risk three year olds. *Journal of Psychoeducational Assessments*, 10, 230-239.

Holloway, S.D., Kagan, S.L., Fuller, B., Tsou, L. and Carroll, J. (2001). Assessing child-care quality with a telephone interview [Electronic version]. *Early Childhood Research Quarterly,* 16, 165-189.

Jaeger, E.and Funk, S. (2001). *The Philadelphia child care quality study: An examination of quality in selected early education and care settings.* A technical report submitted to the Improving School Readiness project of the united way of southeastern PA. Retrieved December 2, 2002 from http://psych.sju.edu/faculty/Jaeger/JaegerFunk2001.pdf

Kwan, C. (1997). The effects of environmental variations in day care centres on the development of young children in Singapore. PhD Thesis. University of London.

Kwan, C., Sylva, K. and Reeves, B. (1998). Day care quality and child development in Singapore. *Early Child development and Care*, 144, 69-77.

Lera, M.J., Owen, C. and Moss, P. (1996). Quality of educational settings for four-year-old children in England. *European Early Childhood Education Research Journal*, 4(2), 21-33.

McCartney, K., Scarr, S., Phillips, D., Grajek, S. and Schwartz, J.C. (1982). Environmental differences among day care centres and their effects on children's development. In E.F. Ziegler and E.W. Gordon (Eds.), *Day Care: Scientific and Social Policy issues.* Boston, MA: Auburn House.

Melhuish, E.C., (1994). What affects the quality of care in English playgroups? *Early Development and Parenting,* 3(3),135-143.

Peisner-Feinberg, E. and Burchinal, M. (1997). Relations between pre-school children's child care experiences and concurrent development: The Cost, Quality and Outcomes Study. *Merrill Palmer Quarterly*, 43(3), 451-447.

Phillips, D., McCartney, K. and Scarr, S. (1987). Child care quality and children's social development. *Journal of Applied Developmental Psychology,* 23(4), 537-543.

Phillips, D., Scarr, S. and McCartney, K. (1987). Dimensions and effects of child care quality: The Bermuda study. In D. Phillips (Ed.), *Quality in child care: What does research tell us?* NAYEC Monograph Series, vol. 1, Washington, DC: National Association for the Education of Young Children.

QCA (2000), *The Foundation Stage Curriculum Guidance.* London, Qualifications and Curriculum Guidance Association.

Rossbach, H.G., Clifford, R.M. and Harms, T. (1991). *Dimensions of learning environments: cross national validation of the Early Childhood Environment Rating Scale*. Paper presented at the annual meeting of the American Educational Research Association, Chicago, IL.

Sammons, P., Sylva, K., Melhuish, E., Siraj-Blatchford, I., Taggart, B. and Elliot, K. (2002) *Measuring the impact of pre-school on children's cognitive progress over the pre-school period. Technical Paper 8a.* London: Institute of Education.

Sammons, P., Sylva, K., Melhuish, E., Siraj-Blatchford, I., Taggart, B. and Elliot, K. (in press). *Measuring the impact of pre-school on children's social behavioural development over the pre-school period.Technical Paper 8b.* London: Institute of Education.

Scarr, S., Eisenberg, M. and Deater-Deckard, K. (1994). Measurement of quality in child care centers. *Early Childhood Research Quarterly,* (9), 131-151.

Siraj-Blatchford, I. (2002a) Final annual evaluation report of the Gamesley Early Excellence Centre. Unpublished report, London, Institute of Education.

Siraj-Blatchford, I. (2002b) Final annual evaluation report of the Thomas Coram Early Excellence Centre. Unpublished report, London, Institute of Education.

Siraj-Blatchford, I., Sylva K., Muttock, S., Gilden, R. and Bell, D. (2004)c) *Researching Effective Pedagogy in the Early Years.* Research Report 356 Department for Education and Skills, Nottingham.

Swaminathan, M. *et al.* (2000) *The Tamil Nadu Early Childhood Environmental Rating Scale (TECERS),* Chennai, India, M.S. Swaminathan Research Foundation.

Sylva, K., Siraj-Blatchford, I., Melhuish, E., Sammons, P., Taggart, B., Evans, E., Dobson, A., Jeavons, M., Lewis, K., Morahan, M. and Sadler, S. (1999). *Characteristics of the centres in the EPPE sample: Observational profiles. Technical Paper 6.* London: Institute of Education.

Sylva, K. (2001). Adapting the Early Childhood Environment Rating Scale (ECERS) to Other Countries and Cultures. Paper presented at the 82nd Annual Meeting of the American Educational Research Association, Seattle.

Tietze, W., Cryer, D., Bairrao, J., Palacios, J., and Wetzel, G. (1996). Comparisons of observed process quality of early child care and education in five countries. *Early Childhood Research Quarterly*, 11(4), 447-475.

Whitebook, M., Howes, C. and Phillips, D. (1989). *Who cares? Child care teachers and the quality of care in America.* Final report on the National Child Care Staffing Study. Oakland, CA: Child Care Employee Project.